The Angel in the Big Pink Hat

By the author

Your Life In the Palm of Your Hand
The Millennium Effect
The Intuitive Advantage

The Angel in the Big Pink Hat

Kathryn Harwig

Spring Press • Minneapolis

Cover illustration: Sheryl Vanderpol
Book design: Dorie McClelland
Published by: Spring Press, 8549 Forestview Ln. N.,
  Maple Grove, MN 55369
  www.harwig.com

   1. Harwig, Kathryn
   2. Mediums, United States
   3. Spiritualism
   4. Title

   BF 1283.H 2005
   133.9-dc21

ISBN 0-9638822-4-4

This book is dedicated to
the thousands of students and clients
who have given me
support, love, and encouragement
over the years.
Thank You.

CONTENTS

Introduction   *vii*

MY DREAM   *1*

What friends are for   *9*
Show time   *15*
The reluctant patient   *23*
Tricks of the Spirit   *27*
Enough healing already!   *33*
But I hate to pack   *37*
Work in the Spirit realm   *41*
You can have it all (but do you want it?)   *47*
You can run . . .   *51*
 . . . But you cannot hide   *57*
Just because you learn something, doesn't mean you
    don't have to learn it again   *61*
The angel in the big pink hat   *65*
Testing that free will stuff   *71*
I never did have a sense of direction   *75*
Souvenirs of the trip   *79*
Kicked out of heaven   *83*

INTRODUCTION

On August 31, 2004, I experienced a dream that has changed my outlook, my soul, and my life. At the time of this dream, I had experienced a very busy, and somewhat traumatic, few months. I had just conducted two back to back workshops, had a very busy consultation schedule, bought a new house and was still trying to sell the old one, been on the radio and was teaching weekly classes. I was also writing a new book, maintaining a web site and answering dozens of e-mail and phone messages a day. I was physically, emotionally, and spiritually exhausted.

As a professional intuitive and medium, I had developed a regular following and a certain amount of acclaim. Rather than feeling joy about this, I had started to feel burdened. There seemed to be a never ending supply of people wishing to speak to a loved one who had passed or to have "psychic" advice about their lives. I loved my work, and was good at it, yet the days were growing heavy on me.

I once read that everyone has a personal "mantra" or saying which they silently repeat to themselves. As we repeat this saying to ourselves many times a day, it becomes a type of self fulfilling prophecy. Some people, for example, might repeat over and over negative mantras, such as "nothing ever works out for me" or "no one cares about me." Other people might use more positive mantras like "I am protected," or "everything works for the best."

In the summer of 2004, my personal mantra had turned into "you can do this Kathryn." I found myself repeating it to myself many times a day. Life had turned into a struggle that I had to get through, rather than a gift to be cherished. I had wonderful friends and a loving relationship and family. I traveled to exotic locations and had satisfying and fulfilling work. I had sufficient money to do whatever I desired. I was relatively healthy. Yet, life felt difficult.

A few weeks before this dream, I had conducted a manifestation workshop. The goal of the workshop was to discover who you really are, and then live your life accordingly. If you become who you truly are, you will get what that type of person gets. It turned out to be a case of "be careful what you teach, you just might listen to yourself." Since that workshop I had been struggling with who I was and what I wanted.

Then came the dream. It was unlike any other dream I have ever had. I am a person who dreams vividly and in vibrant color. Yet never had I experienced a dream so real and detailed. And, the memory of it has stayed with me to this day.

As soon as I awoke the next morning I went directly to my computer and typed my memory of the dream in as much detail as possible. I knew on some gut level that I had been on a transformational journey and that it would change my life. But, I had no idea of the dream's meaning.

I decided to ask my guides for aid in helping me understand the meaning of my dream.

Everyone has guides, but most people are either unaware of them or do not know how to contact their guides. Because of my work, I had become very used to conversing with my guides, who call themselves the Light Collective. They had been aiding me in doing my intuitive work for many years and also were available to help me in my day to day life. I trust them and their information and I knew they could help me to analyze and understand my dream, if I merely asked them to do so. (Guides, just like human friends, need to be asked if you want their assistance. Only in extreme emergencies will they step in without an invitation.)

This is the story of what I learned. My guides assured me that this was NOT just a dream. They told me I was transported to the Spirit realm, to experience healing, learn lessons and to see for myself the place where souls reside between lives.

As a medium, I have talked to a great many souls on the other side. They have told me of their lives there and have tried to describe how it feels to be alive in Spirit. But, until I experienced it for myself,

I could not possibly understand the magnitude, challenge and beauty of that experience.

I believe that what happened to me was completely and totally REAL. Whether I physically left my body and traveled to the Spirit realm or whether it was a dream of a trip to that realm is a question that I cannot answer. In truth, I do not believe that it matters.

I only know, on a very solid and concrete level, that this was a trip that changed my life and showed me things I needed to know. I first wrote of this experience for myself so that I could understand what happened. But, it became clear to me that much of what was revealed to me is relevant to other people. So, here, I share my very personal and sometimes embarrassing and amusing trip to the world of Spirit. The next short chapter is the exact transcript of the dream as typed the following morning. I have left it in its rough form so that you can first read it in all its confusion.

In later chapters, I discuss what my guides have explained to me about what I experienced. Each chapter is headed by a segment of the dream. After each segment, I explain what the Light Collective told me about that piece of the dream. I also have added stories and information that I have garnered over the years in my work as a medium.

This dream has truly transformed me and shown me in a very concrete way that there is a place where our souls go after death to play, create, learn, heal, and, most of all . . . to LIVE. My wish is that the telling of this tale will touch your soul as it has touched mine.

My Dream

My Dream

8-31-04
7:30 A.M.

I dreamed that I went to what appeared to be a new age expo or fair. I was supposed to meet a group of friends and leave for a trip, but instead one of my friends dropped me off there. The hours posted said it hadn't started yet, but there were lots of people there. When I went to pay, they said, "No, just walk in, you have already paid."

The minute I walked in there was a show or pageant being performed and lots of people were watching it. It was very beautiful with beings like fairies and mythical creatures and everyone was watching. I stood and watched it for awhile but I thought, "I have seen this hundreds of times before."

I wandered into the healing area, where there were dozens of healers sitting waiting for clients. They weren't busy because everyone was watching the show. They were all waiting. I didn't want a service but one person came up and said, "You are Kathryn Harwig . . . come with me."

She was a very heavy weight woman and she told me to sit on her lap. Then she just touched various places on my body. She was very strict and seemed irritated that I needed so much healing. She laid me down and another woman came up and said, "You are Kathryn Harwig," and she moved my feet and arms. I was annoyed that everyone knew who I was and thought, "This is why I don't go to expos." Another healer laughed as if she heard me think and said, "We know everyone." I realized I was being arrogant.

The heavy woman took me somewhere else where there was a dog and a lamb. I realized I was only dressed in a short purple gown with nothing under it and the dog and the lamb knew it. The lady who was with them (another healer) laughed and said, "Don't dress that way if you don't want them looking."

By this time my body was very relaxed and I could not concentrate well. The heavy lady gave me a bag (like a makeup bag) of things I needed for a trip. She said I was taking a long trip and would need it. I didn't open it. She also gave me some sort of pill. I paid her $28.

Then I left the healing place and started to walk around the expo. There were people making all sorts of marvelous art everywhere but I kept walking.

At one point I lost an earring and I was looking for it. I looked down and found it but there were two earrings plus a necklace. Then, suddenly, there were hundreds and hundreds of pieces of jewelry all over the floor. When I saw that I knew I really didn't need any jewelry so I left it all and walked on.

I was in a daze. The next thing I came upon was a woman, sort of a shaman doing some sort of performance. There were lots of people watching her but I knew I didn't want to watch. I walked past but there were people blocking my path. They were doing a type of massage with clay and dirt and I sat and watched them. They asked if I wanted a turn and I said yes, so I watched them work until it was my turn. Then they rubbed my feet and hands with salt and sand. It felt wonderful and when I was done they told me to go back to the female shaman.

She called me on stage . . . many people were watching. She waved her hands and asked me if I smoked. I said no, but then remembered I had been at a very smoky fire recently. She said I had asthma but it was okay. She said be careful of smoke. Then she said, "Do you want to know who your arch angel is?" I said no, because I thought she would charge me. (I didn't like her and I didn't like all those people watching this.) She laughed and handed me a sort of paddle that had a funny painting on it of a woman. Under the painting it read "the angel in the big pink hat."

I left and walked away and someone stopped me and said, "You left before it was done . . . you shouldn't do that." But, I knew I could.

Then I had to go to the bathroom but made a wrong turn into a linen room. The person in charge of that room was very small and sort of deformed. He said, "You made a wrong turn," and pushed me out.

Finally, I decided to look into the bag given to me by the large woman healer. There were two pairs of eyeglasses . . . very funny looking ones. One pair was big and would fit over my regular glasses, I thought. The other pair was very tiny. Also, there was a big bottle of pills that said something on the label about how often to take them and I thought, "That is too often." And there were several tubes of lipstick.

I knew it was time to leave even though there was music playing that I wanted to hear. I was so relaxed and disoriented I was afraid I could never leave if I didn't go soon. As I left, the heavy woman walked by me and stuck another pill in my mouth.

Then I woke up. I felt extremely groggy and my body was sore, but a good sore, as if I had been massaged or I had exercised very hard. I knew this dream was important and I remembered so many details that I typed it up immediately.

What friends are for

I dreamed that I went to what appeared to be a new age expo or fair. I was supposed to meet a group of friends and leave for a trip, but instead one of my friends dropped me off there. The hours posted said it hadn't started yet, but there were lots of people there. When I went to pay, they said, "No, just walk in, you have already paid."

ecause of the kind of work that I do, I have spoken at and attended many so-called new age expos. I actually find them rather unpleasant, as I am a little confused and disoriented by the amount of people and the energy that emanates from the attendees, displays, speakers and musicians. There are many booths from which people sell products, goods and services ranging from crystals, to massages, to magic wands. Some of it is beautiful. Much of it is tacky. And all of it works to create a cacophony of noise, energy, and music. Some people are there strictly to sell goods, others to do readings, some set up massage tables and do short healings. In addition, there are various speakers on just about every imaginable topic. The result, to me, is a little like going to a 300-ring circus where everyone is performing at the same time.

"Why," I asked my guides, "would I dream of going to an expo. I would much prefer to dream of a trip."

"Your dream was not of an expo, Kathryn," they replied. "Your dream took you to the realm of Spirit. The place between lives."

I was confused. "If I truly went to the Spirit realm," I asked my guides, "Why would it appear as a new age expo?" They explained this to me.

When we go to the world of Spirit, it always appears in a form that is recognizable to us. When we first go to Spirit, we are disoriented and a little confused. It is, after all, a rather disconcerting experience. So, we see the "other side" in terms that are familiar. Everyone speaks our language, the dress is what we expect, and the setting matches something from the life which we just left.

A devout Christian might go to the classic heaven, perhaps even seeing angels with wings sitting around on clouds. A Buddhist would very likely enter a world of Wats and temples and the language, of course, would not be English. People who expect or believe in nothing after death have a surprise coming for them. They will arrive though, in a place that is understandable and comfortable for them. In other words, my guides said, the Spirit world is pretty much as we expect it to be.

"And why would I expect an expo, of all things?" I asked a tad petulantly. "Well," they explained, "where do you normally go for healing and teaching of a spiritual nature?"

They had a point. While I do not particularly enjoy going to new age fairs or expos, I do think of them as a sort of "one-stop shopping center" where I can experience a number of teachings and products, try on new ideas, take what I like and leave the rest. For me, it is a perfect analogy of what it must feel like to die and awaken into a familiar and yet slightly disorienting environment.

"But I did not experience a white light or have anyone meet me," I added. Having talked to many souls, I know that this is a very common experience for them upon death. My guides reminded me that I did not die, nor did I have a near death experience. I went directly to "Go" (in Monopoly terms) for the purpose of learning a few things and experiencing some healing. Most souls, they assured me, do in fact have a sense of peace and light upon death. They are then met by a loving presence or two (again, for that sense of familiarity). I have been told of these things and believe them to be true, but they were not part of my dream experience. I was merely a visitor for a brief time.

I laughingly realized that rather than having loved ones meet me, I had one drop me off at the door. Of course, I was embarrassed to admit, my close friends were aware of my life struggles. I had been hijacked and dumped into Spirit to learn a few things. It was, no doubt, exactly what I needed to have happen. I had experienced a spiritual intervention and had been forced into "treatment." I would, in all likelihood, not have gone on my own. After all, I was busy. I had a trip to go on. The expo wasn't open yet. I had a whole list of reasons for not going.

But, that is what friends are for. My friend dropped me off with loving intent. No doubt knowing that the trip could wait and that if I was ready to enter, the guard would let me in.

And let me in he did. "You have already paid," he said.

The truth is, we don't have to earn our way into the Spirit realm. No amount of good works (or bad for that matter) will pay our way in. We can't get there by meditating a whole bunch or reading every book that has ever been published. We can't force our way in through intention or holiness or power. It doesn't matter how we lived or how we died. Death by suicide or heart attack or abortion or a car crash makes no difference as to whether or how we enter Spirit. Being a president or a mass murderer or a priest is irrelevant as well. We get in by the grace of the being many call God. Now, what happens when we are in, well, that is another chapter.

Show time

The minute I walked in there was a show or pageant
being performed and lots of people were watching it.
It was very beautiful with beings like fairies and mythical
creatures and everyone was watching. I stood and watched
it for awhile but I thought, "I have seen this hundreds of
times before."

fter a time of rest and greetings by loved ones and guides, the deceased enters into what many call a life review. Like everything in Spirit (and on earth for that matter) no one is forced to do anything. God (or as I shall call it, the Divine) never forces us to do anything. For the Divine is pure love.

But, sooner or later, the deceased decides to do a life review. Why? Because it is necessary to do in order to continue on with all the other wonderful things that the realm of Spirit has to offer. As a medium, I occasionally am asked to talk to a spirit who has not yet started his or her life review. They generally have very little to say because they have not yet started their true lives in the Spirit realm. Sometimes they wish to stay for a time basking in the light of the Divine and spending time with the loved ones who first met them at death's veil. They may stay there for some time, but sooner or later, almost everyone decides to do a life review. The alternative is a pleasant but very inactive rest period. And the one unifying characteristic of the human race is our overwhelming desire to grow.

Life review is a time when the deceased is shown his or her life from start to finish, from all different perspectives. Many of us have heard the term "life flashing before my eyes." A life review is like that, except much more complex.

Most of us believe that we are independent beings and are separate from all other entities and beings. We may form relationships, fall in love, have friendships and enemies. But, all in all, we believe we end at our skin. Because of that, we often feel a sense of loneliness or disconnectedness. As someone described it to me recently: "I feel incomplete, as if I had a hole in my soul."

She does not, of course, have a hole in her soul. What she has is an intuitive knowing that we are all one. Her awareness of our oneness with all beings is in conflict with what we are told here on earth, and this conflict causes a sense of dis-ease. Her sense of separation is not accurate, but it is what we are currently being taught here at earth school.

The reality, which we re-learn when we return to Spirit, is that we are connected to everything.

Returning to Spirit is similar to a drop of water being returned to the ocean. The drop continues to have its own personality and characteristics, but it is also part and inseparable from something huge and powerful.

The life review then becomes a fascinating time when we see not only a re-run of our own life, but the way our soul is intertwined with everything that is. We see our lives from start to finish as experienced by everyone and everything we touched. The clerk you once smiled at, the bird you set free, your coworkers, your first grade teacher, your loved ones and your enemies. And yes, that takes a long time . . . but there is no time in Spirit.

If there is a hell, it might be the emotions that a soul may experience during a life review. Imagine, for example, being a suicide bomber who is watching what it feels like to be killed over and over, knowing you were the cause of all that pain. Or a child abuser, who, in life review, actually lives the life of the child that was hurt.

But, for most of us, life reviews are a time of great joy. We experience the love that others felt for us. We understand petty misunderstandings from another point of view. We feel the total devotion and unconditional love of our pets. And, yes, we feel the compassion and hurt of the earth itself and the mostly unseen mystical beings that inhabit our world.

Which brings us to the play I watched for a short time in my dream. My guides told me that what I saw was actually part of my own (someday to be held) life review. Because of my connection to fairies and mystical beings, I was seeing only a tiny portion of what someday I will watch in great detail.

"Why did I leave then?" I asked. "It was so beautiful to see."

"Because it was not yet your time, you were only a tourist in the Spirit realm," was the answer.

"But, I felt as if I had seen it before," I replied.

All of us live many lifetimes. We are, after all, eternal beings. We tend to hang out with the same group of souls. Some of them chose to incarnate at the same time as we do. Others are not ready yet and stay in Spirit. Still others join us in a disincarnate way and act as our guides, available to remind us of things we have forgotten.

No one is ever forced to return to earth. And

there are many other dimensions in which we can
live. (Remember the words of Jesus: "I have worlds
you know not of.") Yet, sooner or later, most of us
chose to return in a new life to earth school. We
come back because we wish to grow, as all living
beings desire. Perhaps, in our life review, we learned
that we were cruel to our children. We may someday
make an agreement with those souls to trade places
so that we can heal our relationship with them. Or,
we may decide to return to earth as an abused child
in order to experience what that felt like. Perhaps we
will return again as a parent with an abiding desire to
be kind. Or we might choose a life of service to make
amends for our cruelty.

It is always our choice. We live in a free will
universe. But, when we are ready (usually after
several hundred earth years) we generally decide
to return for more lessons.

"And the fairies I saw?" I asked impatiently.

"They are your friends. You have known them
for thousands of years," my guides replied. "They
live much longer than you do in human form. You
saw them in your dream as a happy memory but did

not go to the Spirit realm to revisit your relationship with them."

"So, then," I asked, tapping my foot, "Are you going to tell me why I DID go to Spirit?"

The reluctant patient

I wandered into the healing area, where there were dozens of healers sitting waiting for clients. They weren't busy because everyone was watching the show. They were all waiting. I didn't want a service but one person came up and said, "You are Kathryn Harwig . . . come with me."

After we finish our life review, we are given an opportunity to be healed. Many of the beings who act as healers are in our soul group and know us intimately. Many older souls choose to spend their time in Spirit acting as healers for more newly passed persons. The healing is not, of course, physical, as our bodies are healed of all physical ailments immediately upon passing. But, we still retain our memories, our shame, our addictions, our guilt and our fear.

The life review will bring up many more memories and feelings, both of love and fear. The healers are there to help us learn to focus on love.

Healing, like all things in Spirit (and on earth) is totally voluntary. I was told that, unfortunately, some spirits do not wish to give up their anger or their fear. Sometimes they wish to carry those emotions back to earth so that they can use those emotions to exact revenge. Usually they do so by taking on the persona of the very thing or person that they hated in their last life. Much of the war and carnage so prevalent in our world today is because of this. These souls reincarnate too soon, choosing to return to earth before they have finished healing. Sometimes they return without even finishing their life review.

It is ironic and sad to think that today's terrorists could very well have been victims of a war camp fifty years ago. "Anytime you see a person on a crusade, Kathryn," my guides said, "it is likely that they are reacting to being on the opposite side in a prior life." Strong emotions of any sort, especially when acted upon, are almost always because of an unfinished life review and/or healing.

While I find this very tragic in terms of world affairs, the understanding of that principle should give us compassion for all. The fundamentalists, crusaders, terrorists, and closed-minded folk of our world were perhaps once on the very side of the issue they now so despise.

"But," I asked, "You said I came here to be healed."

"No," they replied, "you were dropped off to be given the opportunity to be healed. You had the choice at the moment they said your name to refuse and leave."

I remembered my dream as if it was still happening. I had been very reluctant to take a healing. I felt vulnerable and afraid. As a matter of fact, I felt that I had been boxed into a corner where I could not refuse. To do so would have been to be rude, and being rude is a difficult thing for me to do. Spirit can be tricky like that. I would learn just how tricky very soon.

Tricks of the Spirit

She was a very heavy weight woman and she told me to sit on her lap. Then she just touched various places on my body. She was very strict and seemed irritated that I needed so much healing. She laid me down and another woman came up and said, "You are Kathryn Harwig," and she moved my feet and arms. I was annoyed that everyone knew who I was and thought, "This is why I don't go to expos." Another healer laughed as if she heard me think and said, "We know everyone." I realized I was being arrogant.

Being healed can be a very scary thing. The first and most frightening step is to be painfully honest about what needs to be healed. Most of us are not terribly fond of inventories of our defects, whether done by us or by anyone else. So, my guides told me, Spirit has a habit of putting us in circumstances in which our fears are shown to us. These lessons are like mirrors. We are shown ourselves as we really are.

One of the rules of the Cosmos is "as above, so below." And, of course, the reverse is also true. The healing done in the Spirit realm is very similar to the way we are healed on earth.

When I teach intuition, I first stress the importance of asking a good question. Often the very kernel of the answer is imbedded in the question. Because of this, many people are hesitant to ask specific questions. It is safer to ask, "Do you have a message for me?" It is much more vulnerable to ask, "What can I do to improve my marriage?" In much the same fashion, the essence of healing is to discover what needs to be healed.

In my healing in the Spirit realm, I was shown in

a gentle way (mostly) the emotional and spiritual wounds from which I needed to be healed. These wounds were causing me physical problems on the earth plane.

My lessons came quickly. I remember feeling very judgmental toward the heavy woman because of her appearance. Of course, in the Spirit realm, souls can chose to look as they wish. Often, I have clients come to see me who wish to speak to a deceased loved one. Sometimes, the loved one will appear to me as being much younger than their age at their death. Other times, they will be more slender or healthy looking. But, they always seem to keep enough distinguishing characteristics that I can identify them for their friends and family.

In one case, I met with a woman whose college age daughter had been tragically killed in a house fire. The young woman who died appeared to me as a child of about seven years of age. When I asked why that was, I was told that she was currently spending her time in Spirit learning how to play and enjoy life and had chosen that appearance for that purpose.

I was told that the heavy-set healer had created her appearance as a mirror for me. My family has a history of weight problems and, without really being aware of the fact, I had developed a fear and a judgment about that issue. My first lesson from the healer was simple. My judgment of others gets in the way of things that aid me. Judgment, I was told, has been a challenge for me throughout my life. I know on an intellectual level that making judgments (whether for good or bad) clouds intuitive information. When I do intuitive consultations I attempt not to make any judgments. I tell people information is not good or bad, it just is. My dream showed me, however, that in my life, my judgments of myself and others have been keeping me from getting what I want and need. If I had allowed my judgment of the heavy woman to get in the way of my healing, I could not have proceeded any further.

My second lesson was about boundaries. I was asked to sit in the lap of a woman I did not know. I was also bothered by the fact that the healers seemed to know more about me than I knew about them. I learned that my extreme need for boundaries on the earth plane has kept me from true intimacy. While setting boundaries is important, it can also be used to maintain a sense of separateness or specialness that keeps us apart from others. Along with that was my need to be in control. In my dream, I was definitely NOT in control of the healing. It bothered me. Another mirror of the way I maintain my artificial belief in the separateness of all beings.

But, the thing that annoyed me the most was that they knew my name. In my dream, I believed I was being recognized as an author and speaker (which happens to me quite often in "real life"). This is both flattering and fearful for me. My issue of "being public" or "being known" was raised very quickly.

Spirit has an interesting way of teaching gently. "We know everyone," was all they said. And, of course, that is true in Spirit. I was no one special. I was not unique. I was not separate. I was part of the whole of the Cosmos. Not better, not worse, just a drop of water in the ocean of Spirit.

Enough healing already!

The heavy woman took me somewhere else where there was a dog and a lamb. I realized I was only dressed in a short purple gown with nothing under it and the dog and the lamb knew it. The lady who was with them (another healer) laughed and said, "Don't dress that way if you don't want them looking."

his part of my dream at first reminded me of a typical fear dream. Most people have had dreams in which they appear somewhere in only their under-wear or even naked. Psychologists say this is an insecurity dream. But, my guides reminded me once again of my fear of being public.

One of the biggest challenges of my career is my ability to shoot myself in the foot just when I am about to become well known or public. In this lesson, Spirit reminded me of another universal rule—I am responsible for what happens to me.

One of the rules of the Cosmos given to me by the Light Collective (my guides) is that "We are Responsible." It is very tempting on earth to blame other people, things, and circumstances for our situa-tions. But, once we realize that we have chosen our lives, this attempt to shift responsibility to someone or something else does not aid us. We are responsible for our lives. We chose them, no matter what the circumstances. And we came to earth to learn the lessons we choose to learn from those lives.

In my dream, I was shown that I had a choice. I could decide not to do anything which caused me to bring attention to myself. I could hide in my home if I wished. I certainly did not need to write books or appear in the media.

Hiding is tempting for me at times. I have "quit" more times than I care to remember. But, some part of me has a yearning to learn the lesson of being seen. And so I continue to elicit the circumstances which cause this to happen.

And in my dream, I could, of course, have put on some underwear. In real life, I was told that means that I no longer need to sabotage myself. I can create circumstances where I am public without shooting myself in the foot. Like all of life's happenings, it is truly up to me.

"But why the dog and the lamb?" I asked my guides.

"What do they symbolize to you?" they asked back. (They do that a lot . . . it is annoying.)

"Well, I answered, "Lambs are the gentlest of creatures and dogs are the essence of unconditional love."

And then I realized my real lesson. My "audience" was not judging me. They loved me or at least were neutral. The judgment, the harm, the fear causing my difficulties was all coming from me. I was responsible.

But I hate to pack

By this time my body was very relaxed and I could not concentrate well. The heavy lady gave me a bag (like a makeup bag) of things I needed for a trip. She said I was taking a long trip and would need it. I didn't open it. She also gave me some sort of pill. I paid her $28.

t last my healing was over. The session was finished. I paid the heavy-set lady and was given a package to take with me.

"Wait a minute," I said to my guides. "If I am in Spirit, why am I paying the healer? Is money really used in the Spirit realm?"

"Because, Kathryn," they replied. "In your society you do not value things for which you do not pay."

When I first became a full-time intuitive, I left a lucrative law practice behind. While people tend to resent paying lawyers, they fully expect to have to do so. I was surprised at how difficult it was for me to charge for my services as an intuitive. While my rational mind told me that an hour of my time is an hour of my time, I believed that I certainly could not charge the same hourly rate as an intuitive as I did as a lawyer. I felt, and many people told me, that spiritual work should be given for free, or at least on a donation basis. But, I also knew I still had to pay the rent and eat.

So, I thought, what is that saying? Is it saying that our society values legal services higher than intuitive services? Or is it saying that I value my own abilities less now than I did when I practiced law?

I remembered the lesson I had just learned. I am responsible. The Light Collective seldom says things sloppily. Their words were "YOU do not value things for which you do not pay." I was somewhat floored to discover that I was actually a little embarrassed by my profession and that I did not place as large a value on it as I had upon being a lawyer.

But, we are all one, I remembered. All work is equally valuable. I smiled. The healer had taught me yet another lesson by charging such a silly amount.

"Why $28.00?" I asked.

"So you would remember it," they said. (Moral: sometimes there is no great cosmic lesson in things.)

I almost didn't ask my guides about what the "long trip" meant. At that time I was preparing to take a group to Egypt and I had just recently returned from Peru. Traveling is my passion and I have been just about everywhere in the world. If I don't have at least one trip in the planning stage, I get restless.

"The trip for which you were prepared is not a

physical journey," the Light Collective volunteered. "It is for your voyage home to your earth world."

I was puzzled. I am by nature very curious. I wondered why I had not opened the bag immediately.

"Because," they simply stated, "You were not yet ready to return."

Work in the Spirit realm

Then I left the healing place and started to walk around the expo. There were people making all sorts of marvelous art everywhere but I kept walking.

Just about everyday I see people who wish to speak to their loved ones who have passed. Perhaps the most common question they ask is, "Does s/he watch over us?" or "Does s/he know what we are doing?"

Most people seem to think that souls in the Spirit realm have nothing better to do than sit and watch those of us on earth. Nothing could be further from the truth.

Now, please do not misunderstand me. Spirits retain their memories of their past lives and they still very much love and care about those of us who remain on earth. They try very hard to keep in touch with us. They do visit and even attempt to communicate, to the best of their ability to do so, and our ability to hear them. But, the best analogy I can use is that it is rather like having a loved one leave on a very exciting and wonderful vacation. They try very hard to stay in touch and to show up for our special occasions. They love to take our phone calls (communications). But, they are having a marvelous and exciting new life and look forward to seeing us very soon when we join them.

The Spirits with whom I have spoken tell me that, sooner or later, they decide they wish to be productive. Just as on earth, souls feel a need to do satisfying work. They aren't required to, of course, as all of their needs and desires are met. But, the one unifying thing about all living things is a need to grow and learn.

After a soul goes through a period of rest and meeting with his or her soul group, the life review, and the healing, the soul then finds itself in a veritable wonderland of opportunity. As I mentioned, some souls decide to become healers, some greeters of the newly passed, others work with specific groups (for example, children or suicide victims).

As Jesus taught us, "In My Father's house are many mansions." In the Spirit realm there are more places to visit and work and learn than we can possibly imagine. Many spirits I have talked to have told me about exploring their earthly interests, whether it be physical sports, astronomy, or science. They tell me the libraries and information in the Spirit realm can keep them occupied for eons.

In addition, there are other dimensions and beings beyond our imagining to which we, as spirits, have access. The Light Collective, my guides, come from a dimension where nothing is totally solid, communication is done by telepathy (mind to mind contact) and Light is the prevailing energy source.

In my dream, I walked by a place where many souls were creating incredible works of art. My heart yearned to join them. In my dream the sculptures could dance, the paintings were vivid and five-dimensional. I was told that all these things were created by the very thinking of them. The power of the mind made them manifest.

"You often spend time here when between lives," my guides told me. "Your sculptures could become living things. Sometimes you would spend centuries molding a star and setting it to spin."

I remember it being hard for me to walk past such a temptation. It is comforting to know that on my return to Spirit I can go back to my work. In the meantime, I plan to once again take classes in sculpture here on the earth plane. Seeing that place in my dream made me more fully understand why I felt so at home with a piece of clay in my hands.

Some souls speak to me of creating music so glorious that all of the realm is transfixed for a time. Others tell me of traveling the galaxy and even other dimensions in awe and wonder at the beauty of creation.

Life in Spirit is rich and full. We do not merely sit around on clouds playing harps. Life after the earth plane has its challenges, its lessons, its joys, and its work. Just as life here on earth does. As above . . . so below.

You can have it all
(but do you want it?)

At one point I lost an earring and I was looking for it.
I looked down and found it but there were two earrings
plus a necklace. Then, suddenly, there were hundreds
and hundreds of pieces of jewelry all over the floor.
When I saw that I knew I really didn't need any jewelry
so I left it all and walked on.

n the Spirit realm (and in the earth plane actually) matter and appearance and all things physical are created by intent and imagination. Over and over again when I do medium work, the deceased tell me that they can look however they wish. In many years of talking to deceased souls, not one has shown up deformed or bloody or even sick looking. That is a strictly Hollywood interpretation of what a "ghost" looks like.

Sometimes older souls do show up looking the age at which they passed. They often explain that they do that so that I can describe their appearance to their loved ones. But, they say, they really don't chose to look that way all the time. It is an amazing realm where you can change your appearance as easily as we change our clothing.

In the same fashion, any material possession or tool or instrument can be created by the mere thought of it. In my dream, I lost an earring. I actually very seldom wear jewelry anymore, even though I have quite a few nice pieces. I was not really upset about losing the actual earring, but I knew it was somewhat valuable and I needed to find it.

"Why," I asked my guides, "did the jewelry multiply?"

"In Spirit, you can have as much jewelry as you wish Kathryn," was their reply. "But, you really didn't want any of it."

What a strange lesson, I thought. Upon the realization that I could have as much of something as I desired, it lost its appeal to me. Then, it became just sort of a nuisance thing with which to have to fuss.

I have read that the diamond mines of South Africa very carefully control the number of gems that are allowed to be released for sale at any given time. As a matter of fact, diamonds are rather common but, by monitoring the quantity allowed to be sold each year, they can control the price. It seems to be a part of the earth mentality that rare things are far more valuable than common things.

In Spirit, however, abundance is a way of life. Because of that, material things hold very little appeal, except as a way to express creativity and to learn.

"And Kathryn," my guides interjected, "You forgot to say something. As above, so below. Abundance is a way of life on earth as well. You have just forgotten."

You can run . . .

I was in a daze. The next thing I came upon was a woman, sort of a shaman doing some sort of performance. There were lots of people watching her but I knew I didn't want to watch.

Because of the kind of work that I do, most people assume that I am fond of ritual and shamanic work. The truth is, it makes me very nervous. So, I was not happy in my dream when I came upon a female shaman.

There was a rather large crowd around her and I remember carefully skirting my way around the outside of the circle. Do you know what it is like when you are walking through a store or a series of booths at a fair and you don't want to make eye contact in case they start talking to you? That is how I remember acting at this point in my dream.

"What is it," I asked my guides, "that makes me so uncomfortable around ritual? And, since I am, why did I run into that very thing in the Spirit realm?"

"You always tell people, Kathryn," that "all paths lead to the same God."

Oh good, I thought, now they are quoting me back to myself. I hate it when they do that.

"Yes," I agreed. "So what is it about that path that is uncomfortable to me? And why did I need to avoid it?"

Even in the Spirit realm, it is common to be

uncomfortable around the unfamiliar. I grew up in a very conservative fundamentalist Christian church. I can sing Gospel music with the best of them and quote the Bible pretty darn well. But, when it comes to beating a drum or chanting I feel, well, foolish.

Ah, I thought. It was the fear of the unknown. The doubt and skepticism about that which I am unfamiliar.

Many people believe that upon death souls become privy to all the secrets of the universe. They expect me to ask their passed loved ones to predict the future or tell them what to do. Oftentimes, I only get a shrug of the shoulders and a look of compassion from the Spirit. Truth is, spirits are certainly not God, nor even angels. They are deceased and living in a very different world, but still one which functions in many ways just like our earthly world.

Other people come to me wanting to play a game I have labeled "stump the psychic." That consists of a pre-arranged answer that they need to receive from the Spirit before they will believe I am not a fraud.

Now, I am very understanding of that concern. But, the Spirits just aren't often willing to play that game. Imagine going away on a very long trip and not seeing your loved ones in years. You finally have a chance to talk to them. What do you want to say? The usual things, probably. How much you love them. How proud you are. Maybe an apology or a comment on an important event. But, probably, you would be rather annoyed when asked things like, "What do I have in my pocket?" or, "What did you give me for my tenth birthday?"

I fully understand the need people have for verification of my authenticity. I also understand the desire for irrefutable proof of life after death. Unfortunately, that is, at least thus far, impossible.

A few months ago, a family came to me for a consultation. Their son had died under very unusual circumstances. He came through and described to me how his car had been forced off the road by a van. He then explained drowning when he hit a body of water. He asked his father to forgive the van driver (all this was, by the way, later acknowledged by his family as the circumstances of his passing). Near the end, the mother said, "Ask him what I have of his in my purse."

I could see him throw up his hands and sympathetically laugh. There was nothing he or I could do to prove he was still very much alive, happy, and only concerned about the anger the family was still harboring concerning his death.

"So," I said to my guides, "I am doing that? Questioning that which I cannot prove?" They only nodded. (I hate it when they do that, too.)

. . . But you cannot hide

I walked past but there were people blocking my path.
They were doing a type of massage with clay and dirt and
I sat and watched them. They asked if I wanted a turn and
I said yes, so I watched them work until it was my turn.
Then they rubbed my feet and hands with salt and sand.
It felt wonderful and when I was done they told me to go
back to the female shaman.

ometimes, even in the Spirit realm, you need to be pampered a little before you can face the unfamiliar. By this time in my dream, I was confused, disoriented and a little distressed. I had, after all, had a long day (or night as the case may be).

Spirits tell me that there is a resting place. Some souls stay there a long time, merely resting, being with friends, recuperating, maybe even getting a massage for all I know.

Some souls are very tired after living on earth. It is, after all, a school, and a difficult one at that. Sometimes during readings, souls come in only to say they are happy, resting, meeting loved ones, and having tea. We can stay in the resting place as long as we wish and go there whenever we desire. It is a place full of kindness and light and angels.

But sooner or later, we get a little restless (remember that growth and learning thing we all do). Some souls may stay in the resting place for centuries, others for decades or days. But, then, it is time to go out and do a little more growing.

"And that is what happened to me?" I asked my guides.

"When you were ready, you were sent back to face your fear of the unknown," they answered.

"I thought it was a free will place." I asked, "Why couldn't I just go forward? Why did I have to return?"

"In the Spirit realm, just as on earth, there is order and progression. You do not have to do anything. But, if you do not, you will stay where you are," they responded. "Even in Spirit, you cannot skip from kindergarten to college."

Many people ask me if they are "old souls." My standing joke about that is that old souls are just slow learners.

As we have discussed, no one is forced to do anything in Spirit or on earth. We live in a free-will universe with no preordained future. Because the future is not set in stone, I can never tell a person definitely what will happen. All I can ever tell people is the most likely event to occur if things continue as they are as of the day we speak. Everyone has a right to change anything in the future, both here and in Spirit. As I tell people, "If you don't like a certain prediction, go out and do something to change it."

In my dream, I had a choice to stay in the resting

place for a long time, being buffed and polished, rubbed and scrubbed (my personal idea of heaven). But, I choose to return to the shaman, grumbling a bit along the way.

Just because you learn something, doesn't mean you don't have to learn it again

She called me on stage . . . many people were watching. She waved her hands and asked me if I smoked. I said no, but then remembered I had been at a very smoky fire recently. She said I had asthma but it was okay. She said be careful of smoke. Then she said, "Do you want to know who your arch angel is?" I said no, because I thought she would charge me. (I didn't like her and I didn't like all those people watching this.)

asked my guides, "If I was in the Spirit realm, why did she talk about my physical body?"

"Well, Kathryn," they reminded me again, "You are still alive."

Oh yeah. I really hadn't liked being there with the shaman.

I had to admit she had been right about the asthma. It had plagued me as a child but had given me very little trouble for many years. So why bring it up now? And what was this about an arch angel? I was pretty sure it was a ripoff. And besides, having all those people watching while she told me that stuff had made me very uncomfortable.

"Do you see what you are doing Kathryn?" My guides asked.

I shook my head no. All I remembered was that I had wanted out of there as quickly as possible.

"You are repeating the same exact lessons you learned from the healer," my guides continued.

I once heard someone say that if you keep doing what you always do, you keep getting what you always get. I suppose that is as good a definition of karma as I can give. On earth, the word *karma* is used a lot, generally incorrectly. It is not a punishment for past sins. It is simply a lesson we are still learning.

In my intuitive practice, I have noticed that most people have certain areas of their lives which are their "issue" areas. Most people, thank goodness, only have one or two. For example, some people have money issues. Others have relationship or health or addiction issues. I have seen that these areas then become the focus of that person's attention and take on a special importance in that person's life. Because of that focus, they seem to repeat the same behavior over and over again. And, in karmic terms, life after life after life.

I certainly have my own set of issues, as my guides had no hesitancy in pointing out. And, both on earth and in Spirit, I was presented with "opportunities" to look at them, work on them, and, hopefully, leave them behind.

The interesting part of my dream is that I did not see that I was repeating the same behavior with the shaman that I had at the healers.

Once again, I had judged the shaman (maybe she was a fraud . . . maybe she would over charge me). And, I still had been bothered by being public, appearing on stage, and being looked at.

I sighed heavily. "I thought I was healed of those things," I pouted.

"No," my patient guides explained. "But you do now recognize them. That is the first step."

They went on to explain that once we determine the lessons we wish to learn, we then choose circumstances in which to practice them. In other words, I will continue to choose to be in places and situations where being public is possible until such time as I resolve that issue. For people for whom that is not an issue, being public is unimportant. It either happens or it doesn't. Either way, for them it is no big deal.

And that, my friends, is karma. We place ourselves in positions where we run into our issues. Why? Because we are beings who wish to grow and learn.

The angel in the big pink hat

She laughed and handed me a sort of paddle that had a funny painting on it of a woman. Under the painting it read "the angel in the big pink hat."

O ne question that I am asked a lot is: "Do I have a guardian angel?" And, of course, I always answer yes. Everyone is protected by the Divine. It is also true that we all still die (and live, and die, and live and die but I digress).

But, that is a simplistic answer. No one really "has" an angel, as if one has been assigned strictly to you. Angels, according to my guides and the spirits with whom I have spoken, are messengers and helpers of the Divine . . . of God.

There are a "host" of angels. My best understanding of angels is that they have never been and never will be human. They are, in that sense, a different species than we are and are subject to different "rules" and circumstances (kind of like how dogs and cats and cows will never reincarnate as humans).

Now I must admit that I have a very incomplete understanding of angels. Their function and their mission is above and beyond my ability to comprehend. It reminds me of the Taoist statement which says in essence: "The God you can understand is not the true God."

Nor were my guides particularly helpful on this topic. They admit that angels are rather beyond their understanding as well. Which points out a rather interesting thing about guides. They are not all-knowing and all-seeing. They know and see from a very different perspective than do we, but they are still limited. And, like all living things, they are growing and learning themselves.

Understandably, when people come in for intuitive consultations, they want absolute answers. They want to know their guide's name, what s/he looks like, what is absolutely going to happen to them, and so forth. But, the truth is, there is very little that is absolute in this life or in Spirit.

Take, for example, the name of your guide or guides. Most guides are souls you have known in many lives and between lives. They see things from a different perspective and have access to a huge library of information that you don't have here on earth. So, they are very helpful to have around. When I ask guides for their name, they usually laugh and say something like, "He can call me Joseph."

Why is this true? Because we have all had hundreds of names in our many many lifetimes. I am Kathryn in this life. But I have also been Leia and Haa'am and other names I do not remember. In Spirit, we actually recognize each other by our energy signature and names are rather irrelevant.

"Since we cannot understand angels," I said to my guides, "What is this stuff about the angel in the pink hat?"

"Angels are messengers of the Divine," my guides reiterated. They told me to review the Biblical stories where angels appear to people in order to deliver messages, warnings, and sometimes protection. "Angels are agents of the being you call God," they went on to say. "They are not agents of Kathryn." (I hate it when they try to tell jokes.)

As far as my understanding can stretch, angels do not have free will in the same way that we do. They function as emissaries, messengers, and agents of the power of powers, God, the Goddess, the Ultimate, the Divine.

If they "guard" us, they do so because it is the will of God for them to do so. They very seldom will interfere with our free-will decisions. It is pretty obvious that there are a lot of horrible things happening on earth which are not being prevented. There are accidents and suicides and murders and worse. If the work of angels was solely to protect us, we would have to conclude that they do not do a particularly good job.

The Divine is allowing us free will, knowing that we will continue to grow and learn and return to Spirit to be rejuvenated and healed.

"Ok," I said, my head spinning with my inability to comprehend. "But what about the angel with the big pink hat?"

"Oh," they said. "If you see her, ask for a message."

Testing that free will stuff

I left and walked away and someone stopped me and said, "You left before it was done . . . you shouldn't do that." But, I knew I could.

Many people have told me that this is their last lifetime. What they mean, I think, is that they are done playing out some great karmic drama and are ready to move to the Spirit realm on a full-time basis.

I always ask them, "What will you do then?"

We are eternal beings. I am not absolutely certain about much, but I am certain about that. When I was just a small girl, I learned that matter cannot be created or destroyed. This is true of souls as well. You can kill me, hurt me, love me, hate me, and help me. But no one can destroy me. Not even me.

I am, apparently, not yet ready to step off the cycle of life. I asked my guides why I left before it was done (whatever "it" was).

"You chose to remove yourself from the learning cycle in Spirit at that point," was their answer.

"But why?" I asked. "Wasn't there more for me to learn?"

If guides can roll their eyes, they did. "Trust us, Kathryn, you have plenty left to learn."

"But," they went on, "it was time for you to take

your learning back to earth plane. You were, after all, only a tourist in the Spirit realm."

And I left, because I could. That is free will in action.

I never did have a sense of direction

Then I had to go to the bathroom but made a wrong turn into a linen room. The person in charge of that room was very small and sort of deformed. He said, "You made a wrong turn," and pushed me out.

have always had a horrible sense of direction. As a matter of fact, the standing joke in my family is, "If you want to know which way to turn, ask Kathryn, and then turn the other way."

On my way out of the Spirit realm, I ended up in a linen room. The walls were lined with freshly laundered snow-white towels. The attendant in the room was dressed in white and seemed stunted. It was an unpleasant place and I was glad to be pushed out.

Many religions have a tradition of a place between life and the Spirit realm. In the Catholic religion it is called Purgatory, the Buddhists call it the Bardo. It is a place between places. A realm in between realms.

When I asked my guides what the linen room was all about in my dream, they said, "You stumbled into the Bardo."

"Explain." I demanded.

"Some souls do not feel themselves worthy of entering into what they think of as heaven," they told me. "Remember that the Spirit realm appears as you expect it to be. If a soul feels unworthy to enter, upon death it enters a waiting area until it has healed enough to feel worthy to proceed."

"What do they do there?" I asked. "Nothing," was the reply. "It is similar to an airport lounge or a train terminal. When they are ready, they depart."

"What keeps them there?" I asked.

"Their own belief system," was the reply.

"Does that explain the phenomena of ghosts then?" I wondered.

"Most so-called ghosts," my guides responded, "are really just energy loops replaying. The soul is not present but the energy of the event plays over and over like a camera playing a scene in a never ending loop. It is not dangerous and is actually somewhat amusing."

"There are souls, however," they went on, "that refuse to leave the earth plane even for the purpose of going to the light. It is rare, but it does happen. Sometimes they are so disoriented that they do not believe they are dead. They are not dangerous, but they are certainly confused. Sooner or later, they generally figure it out and go on."

"Should we try to help them do so?" I asked.

"Kathryn," they replied. "You could not even find your own way out of the Bardo. Maybe leave that to someone else."

Souvenirs of the trip

Finally, I decided to look into the bag given to me by the large woman healer. There were two pairs of eyeglasses . . . very funny looking ones. One pair was big and would fit over my regular glasses, I thought. The other pair was very tiny. Also, there was a big bottle of pills that said something on the label about how often to take them and I thought, "That is too often." And there were several tubes of lipstick.

s I was leaving, I finally looked into the bag I had been given for my "trip." This contained, my guides told me, all I needed to do my work and live my life back on earth.

"Why two pairs of eyeglasses?" I asked. I could understand the need for glasses, as my vision had been a problem for me in the last few years.

"You are a seer," they replied matter-of-factly. You need to see the small and unseen. And you also might enjoy seeing the large and in plain view."

"And the pills?" I asked. I hadn't really liked the pills. They were large and had to be chewed and tasted like dry grass.

"When you return to earth plane, you return to a physical body. It does you no good to see if your body is not in proper order."

Well, I had to agree with them there. I have a strong tendency to ignore, neglect, and generally beat up my body. Ever since I was a little girl, I felt decidedly uncomfortable in it. It didn't work well, first plaguing me with asthma so I could not run and play like other children. Then shutting down nearly completely at age thirty so that I spent six weeks in intensive care. I couldn't argue that taking care of the body I was using might be a rather good gift for my journey.

But, the lipstick . . . why in the world would I get lipstick?

"For Showtime Kathryn," they laughed. Show time is my other mantra. The one I say to myself when I am going out into the world. And I understood. It was show time. I could hide no more.

So there I had it, the three things I needed to live on earth plane. Vision, Health and Confidence. I smiled at my guides and thanked them for helping me understand.

Kicked out of heaven

I knew it was time to leave even though there was music playing that I wanted to hear. I was so relaxed and disoriented I was afraid I could never leave if I didn't go soon. As I left, the heavy woman walked by me and stuck another pill in my mouth.

The Spirit realm is incredibly beautiful. The music that was playing as I woke up lingered in my mind for days. I didn't want to leave. But, my work and learning are here on earth plane . . . for now. I will return soon enough.

Blessings to all who read this as you traverse this realm and the next.

Kathryn

What People Are Saying

Over the past ten years I have done psychic and spirit communication readings for over five thousand people. In many of these readings, the spirits of deceased loved ones have come through to answer questions and offer love and support. It is from these communications that much of the information in this book has been gathered. I asked a few of my clients to write a short paragraph about how this feels from their perspective. The following quotes are unedited and were gathered to give the reader a taste of what it is like to experience a conversation with a spirit.

One hour with Kathryn Harwig changed my life. I had lost my father to suicide nearly a year before. I had been struggling with his choice and the fact I never had a chance to say goodbye. There was also anger. There were so many answered I needed and so much I wanted to say. Whether you lose someone to suicide or a heart attack, or any other unexpected way, you miss that opportunity for closure. I had never gone to see a channeler before, but someone recommended I see Kathryn to help connect with my father and get some answers.

At first, I admit, I was a bit hesitant. I was nervous too. But as soon as I met Kathryn she put me at ease and started telling me all kinds of things my father wanted me to know. There were so many tears that day. So many questions and so many answers. Kathryn told me things she never could have known unless she truly was channeling my father's thoughts and feelings. I left Kathryn feeling as though I had just spent an hour with my father. It was the most remarkable experience of my life. It is what has helped me in the time that's passed now to move forward and forgive my father. It's that visit that also convinced me that my father is still with me, and will be forever. Knowing that makes the world a better place.

R.K., Atlanta, Georgia

On November 16, 2004, I arrived at my appointment for an intuitive reading with Kathryn. I wasn't quite sure what to expect. I only knew that I was deeply sad about the loss of my little daughter, and I knew she still "lived" in some way and that I wanted very much to contact her. Kathryn had the reputation of being someone who could communicate with loved ones who had crossed over to the other side, who had "gone to spirit."

When I first walked into Kathryn's home, I felt immediately comfortable and surrounded with spiritual presence. There were several statues of the Buddha, which felt right, as my daughter had loved her book called *Buddha and His Friends.* Kathryn's voice was calm and welcoming, and her demeanor was soothing. She clearly understood the importance of this visit to me.

During the reading itself, Kathryn spoke with my child and told me what she wanted me to know. The first thing was that my husband, my child and I had lived several lives together already. My daughter wanted to tell me about the first one, in which we had lived together as part of a spiritual community in the first century A.D. At first, I was a bit impatient, because my pain was very deep and immediate and I wanted to know about the most recent life we had lived with her and why she was gone from that life. Later, however, what she told me about that early life began to mean a lot to me, and is one of the things I listen to when I replay the tape Kathryn made of the reading. We are a Quaker family, and the roots of Quakerism stem from a desire to re-experience the spiritual immediacy of that early century. What Kathryn had told me felt true and real and is something I think about often.

During such readings, there is always a nagging question about authenticity. I wanted some indication that Kathryn knew things about my daughter that she could not have known without communicating with her. Several things she old me about what my child said she remembered experiencing during the accident confirmed this, as well a four possessions that she told Kathryn she wanted us to keep. They were all important things, and one was a rather unusual object—a balloon she had covered with handmade paper that I had hung in the dining room. She was very proud of having made this, and it seemed right that she would want us to keep it.

Parents almost always blame themselves to some extent when something happens to their child, and I was no exception. My husband and I had tormented ourselves, going over every detail, wondering what we could have done. Kathryn reassured me about this, telling me more than once that it was not our fault, there was nothing we could have done, and that our child was fine, that she loved us and was concerned about us.

Probably the most comforting thing about the experience was knowing that Kathryn was speaking directly to my child and telling me what she had said. I had so missed speaking with her, and this was a way I could. Kathryn was one of the few people who spoke of my daughter, and continues to speak of her, in the present tense, as a living being who is busy and active and vibrant. I value her accessibility and patience. Kathryn Harwig does not take lightly the importance of what she tells people who are experiencing something extremely painful. She has managed to illuminate my daughter's life for me as something that goes far beyond the bounds of one particular short earthbound life, and I treasure that.

Malva Cohen, Minneapolis

I have always been interested in the possibility of spirit communication. I knew that if I ever lost someone close to me, I would somehow try to pursue it. In September 2003, the unimaginable happened, and I lost my oldest daughter in a house fire. Losing a child is a pain like no other. How could I go on without someone I loved more than life itself? Then, through a series of truly amazing "coincidences," I met Kathryn Harwig. She gave me what I so desperately wanted and needed, but thought was unattainable—proof of life after death. She showed me that I was still very much connected to my daughter and always would be.

Kathryn proved to me again and again that my

daughter was not only alive, but was also very happy to be in spirit. She described her personality and physical appearance perfectly. She described a family event to me in great detail. She told me things that only my daughter could have told her. Kathryn gave me what I needed not just to live, but to live with joy and love, just as my daughter wants me to. Because of Kathryn's amazing gift, I can be secure in the knowledge that life truly is eternal and that some day my daughter and I will be together again. And for this, I will be forever grateful.

Kim Wenci, Owatonna, Minnesota

When my father passed away, my heart was broken and I had a hard time accepting his death. During a session with Kathryn, she could tell my heart was heavy so she told me the wonderful things my father's spirit was experiencing and also things that he wished for me to know. This was such a comfort to me. Now

I am at peace with his passing and feel closer to him knowing his loving spirit is still with me.

Kathryn has also been a tremendous help in so many other areas of our lives. She has given us insight into our future retirement years, steered us in the right direction in legal matters, and helped with decisions regarding my mother who has Alzheimer's (and helped me understand what she was going through), and made clear health and job issues that have come up. She has also given us insight into personal and spiritual matters. With Kathryn's advice, we are able to make better decisions and are more confident about the results. When talking with her, it is evident she is speaking from the heart and wants only the best for you. When I give her name to friends of mine, I feel like I am giving them a gift—that is what she is—a gift.

Camille Steen, Minneapolis

I went to see Kathryn after losing my son to a "so-called accident." I needed to know if our suspicions were right about it REALLY NOT being an accident. I had never been to a psychic before so did not know what to expect, plus, being a little skeptical of course. When I got there, Kathryn told me there was a man waiting for me and that he had been there about an hour (we were late). I was really surprised and grateful that his Spirit WAS there! I truly believe he was there. There was so much that Kathryn could NOT have known. He told me how his accident REALLY happened. We were RIGHT in it NOT being an accident like the cops tried to pass it off as. He also told us WHO it was that caused it, in which we were RIGHT again! He also talked about having a very angry son, which is very TRUE AGAIN! Kathryn did not even know that he had kids! For those of you who are skeptical, PLEASE, go see Kathryn, she is the REAL deal! My reading was nothing short of AMAZING!

A True Believer, Diane Hagman, Rush City, Minnesota

Kathryn Harwig

Internationally-acclaimed author, speaker, trainer and attorney, Kathryn Harwig has been an intuitive since birth and an attorney since 1982.

Kathryn grew up on a farm in Minnesota, USA, where her intuitive abilities were seen by her parents and neighbors as a surprising and yet accepted skill. She went on to attend the University of St. Cloud, Minnesota, receiving a Bachelor of Science degree (magna cum laude) in Psychology and Sociology.

After graduation she became a probation officer in Minneapolis, Minnesota. For many years she supervised and wrote pre-sentence investigations regarding adult felons. As she worked with the most dangerous of criminals, she came to fully realize the extent that intuition aided her in her awareness and knowledge of others. She then attended the University of Minnesota in a graduate program of Criminal Justice Studies, specializing in the prediction of dangerousness.

In 1982 she graduated cum laude from William Mitchell College of Law with a Doctorate in Law. She was a successful partner in a law firm for many years.

Her first book, *Your Life In the Palm of Your Hand,* was written in 1994. It became an immediate success and a Book-of-the-Month Club selection. Her later books, *The*

Millennium Effect (1996) and *The Intuitive Advantage* (2000) have also received acclaim.

Kathryn has trained thousands of people to use their intuition to maximize their career goals, relationships, and life skills. She works actively with individuals, corporations and police departments.

Kathryn appears regularly on television and radio and often writes columns for newspapers and magazines on intuition and related subjects. In August of 1999 she was featured in a one hour television special on the Arts & Entertainment network's "The Unexplained." In 2003 she appeared in a segment of Court TV's "Psychic Detectives." In November 2003 she was featured on a news special on WCCO television. She is a regular monthly guest on the the Pat Miles show on WCCO radio.

Kathryn has traveled the world presenting this information and has been featured on radio and television in Jamaica, Brazil and Australia, as well as many other places.

Spring Press is dedicated to publishing and promoting books and materials that challenge the mind and spirit. Our books are available through major bookstores and also at www.harwig.com

Phone: 763-315-1904
Fax: 763-425-3672

e-mail: kathrynharwig@aol.com